From Ethel Ray Nance to Kamala Harris:
A Legacy of Equality and Justice
By Karen Felecia Nance

Published by Amazon Books (2025)

© 2025 by Karen Felecia Nance

Printed in the United States of America

All rights reserved. International copyright secured. No part of this book may be reproduced, stored in a retrieval system, or transmitted in any form or by any means, whether electronic, mechanical, photocopying, recording or otherwise, without prior written permission of the publisher, except for inclusion of brief quotations in an acknowledged review.

From Ethel Ray Nance to Kamala Harris: A Legacy of Equality and Justice

by Karen Felecia Nance

A DREAM DEFERRED, A LEGACY ALIVE: HONORING THE PRESIDENCY OF KAMALA HARRIS

Introduction

"From Ethel Ray Nance to Kamala Harris: A Legacy of Equality and Justice" honors the vision of a more inclusive, just America, a dream championed by figures like Ethel Ray Nance and Kamala Harris. Though Kamala Harris and Tim Walz were not elected in 2024, this book refers to them as President and Vice President, recognizing the values they represent and the profound hope they instilled in millions of voters who saw in them the possibility of real, transformative leadership.

In a poignant moment, Jamal Simmons, a former aide to Vice President Harris, publicly called for President Biden to step down near the end of his term, allowing Harris a brief tenure as the first female president of the United States. Though symbolic, this suggestion underscored the aspirations of countless Americans who envisioned Harris breaking barriers at the highest level of leadership—a testament to a dream so vivid that it continues to shape public discourse, even when deferred.

This choice to call her "President Harris" within these pages is intentional, reflecting not only on what might have been but also on the enduring impact of her work and the belief in a future where equity and justice prevail. Langston Hughes' iconic poem "Harlem" asks, "What happens to a dream deferred?" Here, that deferred dream becomes a call to action, reminding us that such aspirations are not forgotten but live on in the spirit of those who continue to push for progress.

Ethel Ray Nance and Kamala Harris, though separated by decades, share a legacy of pioneering justice. They inspire countless others to reach for what Hughes described as a world where a dream "explodes" into reality. In this book, their stories—and those of leaders like Tim Walz—illuminate a pathway forward, a reminder that history's torchbearers may not always hold office, but their influence reverberates across time, bridging past struggles with the collective hope for a more just future. This journey, from Nance to Harris, encapsulates a legacy not denied, only awaiting its moment to fully shine.

DEDICATION

This book is dedicated to my great-grandfather, William Henry Ray, my grandmother, Ethel Ray Nance, and my uncle, Glenn Ray Nance. These extraordinary individuals have left an indelible mark on both history and my heart. Their lives, stories, and unwavering commitment to justice have shaped our shared narrative of humanity and fueled the work I carry on today.

To my great-grandfather, William Henry Ray: Although we never had the opportunity to meet, your strength and perseverance as a civil rights pioneer inspire me daily. Born just three years after the Civil War, you faced a world in which freedom for Black people was newly won yet continuously threatened. Your courage in seeking education and opportunity despite the barriers of racial prejudice speaks volumes about your resilience. Your journey from the oppressive South to the relative safety of the North exemplifies the desire for progress that many African Americans pursued during your time. You laid the foundation for future generations, providing the roots from which we now stand tall. Your legacy remains a guiding light in my life, reminding me to confront injustices and work toward a society where equality is not just an ideal but a reality.

To my grandmother, Ethel Ray Nance: You were a beacon of equality and justice in your time, and your legacy continues to shine brightly today. Born into a world still grappling with racial violence and segregation, you dedicated your life to fighting against these injustices. From becoming Minnesota's first Black female police officer to working with cultural icons like W.E.B. Du Bois, Langston Hughes, Zora Neale Hurston, and Thurgood Marshall, you exemplified the kind of persistence and visionary thinking that drives social change. Your work with the NAACP and your leadership in organizing pivotal events like the *Opportunity* Literary Dinner helped to elevate Black voices at a time when they were often silenced or marginalized. You showed the world the transformative power of Black culture and civil rights advocacy, and your legacy serves as a powerful example of what one person's commitment to justice can achieve.

To my uncle, Glenn Ray Nance: A custodian of family history and a guardian of truth, your invaluable contributions to this book have allowed me to bring the story of Ethel Ray Nance—your mother, my grandmother—to life. Your memories, insights, and dedication to preserving the family's history have ensured that this story is told with authenticity and depth. Through your support, I've been able to trace the legacy of courage, activism, and love that runs through our family's veins.

I also dedicate this book to **President Kamala Harris, Vice President Tim Walz**, and all those who work tirelessly for equity and justice in their daily lives. President Harris, your groundbreaking leadership as the first Black and South Asian woman to serve as Vice President and now as President represents the culmination of generations of struggle, sacrifice, and hope. You embody the dreams, aspirations, and victories of countless individuals who have fought for a more inclusive and equitable society. Your presidency is a testament to the progress we have made, as well as a reminder of the work that still lies ahead.

Vice President Walz, your tireless commitment to addressing systemic inequities, both in Minnesota and across the nation, continues the legacy of activists like Ethel Ray Nance, who believed that true justice requires action at every level of society. Your leadership in advocating for criminal justice reform, educational equity, and economic opportunity for marginalized communities reflects the same spirit of service and dedication that my grandmother exemplified.

To my **podcast guests**, whose voices and stories amplify the ongoing work of equality and justice across the globe: You are the everyday heroes who carry forward the legacies of those who came before us. Your dedication to creating a more equitable world through your work—whether in education, healthcare, the arts, or social justice—reminds us that the fight for justice is never isolated to one person or one moment. Each of you, in your own way, has contributed to the broader movement for justice, and I am honored to have had the opportunity to share your stories with the world. Your courage, determination, and unwavering belief in the power of justice inspire me every day.

I am also deeply grateful for the unwavering support of my **husband, Sheldon**, and my **sons, Adryan and Menelik**. You have stood by me every step of the way, offering love, encouragement, and strength. This journey would not have been possible without your belief in me and your dedication to our family. Sheldon, you have been my rock, and your support has empowered me to continue the work of those who came before us. Adryan and Menelik, you are the future, and it is my hope that this book will serve as a reminder of the legacy you inherit and the responsibility you hold to continue the fight for equality and justice.

Finally, this book is dedicated to everyone who has committed themselves to building legacies of equity and justice. You are the change-makers who, through small acts of courage and large movements for change, ensure that the vision of a more just and compassionate world continues to live and thrive. Your work, often unseen, is vital and deeply appreciated. Together, we carry forward the torch of justice, illuminating the path for future generations.

With deepest admiration and appreciation,
Karen Felecia Nance

ACKNOWLEDGMENT

I would like to extend my deepest gratitude to **Francis Joseph Gallego** for his incredible contribution to writing the foreword for this book and for his diligent work in editing. His insights and careful attention have been invaluable in bringing this project to life, and I am truly grateful for his mentorship and friendship throughout this journey.

I also want to express my heartfelt thanks to **Hylton Maine** for his exceptional work in designing the cover of this book. His artistic vision and creativity have captured the essence of this story, giving it a powerful visual representation that aligns beautifully with the themes of justice and equality explored in these pages.

This book would not have been possible without the support and contributions of both Francis and Hylton, and I am deeply appreciative of their dedication and commitment to this project, which has helped transform an idea into a reality.

With gratitude,

Karen Felecia Nance

Contents

Introduction 4
FOREWARD 12
PREFACE 14
INTRODUCTION 19
Chapter 1: Roots of Resilience 23
Chapter 2 The Duluth Lynchings: A Turning Point for Justice . 32
Chapter 3 Navigating Identity: 39
    The Ray Children and the Burden of Passing 39
Chapter 4: A Turning Point in Activism 45
Chapter 5 The Emmett Till Anti-Lynching Act: A Long-Awaited Victory 53
Chapter 6 Connecting Legacies: Ethel Ray Nance's Minnesota-California Bridge and Kamala Harris's Return 58
Chapter 7 Bridging Legacies & Intersectionality Justice Across Generations 62
Chapter 8. Modern Trailblazers: Continuing the Legacy for Justice and Intersectionality 67
    Advocacy & Justice 67
    Health & Wellness 72
    Entrepreneurship & Innovation 74
    Art, Media & Representation 77
    Education & Cultural Preservation 79
Epilogue Carrying the Torch Forward 81
APPENDIX A 86
APPENDIX B 87

FOREWARD

On November 28, 2022, I had the privilege and immense honor of meeting Karen Nance in Lisbon, Portugal, during the African Lisbon Tour, which focuses on the hidden history of Portugal- one of the leading exporters of enslaved people during the Transatlantic Slave Trade. This tour continued to shed light on the brutalities of white supremacy and colonization. It was a beautiful and bittersweet tour, and I was immediately drawn to Karen and her humility. We instantly connected on our love for history, social justice, and the beauty and rawness of storytelling.

There is such beauty in "talking story" storytelling and being authentic. When we have that ability, or privilege, to write or speak so openly about our history, despite the pain, and with possibility, it becomes such a beautiful art form. Reading Karen's writings allows one to find safety and space because of the importance and need for the elevation of brown and black voices.
Many times, due to our shared history of pain and systems of oppression, our voices were often silenced and whitewashed in society. Karen's writing about her grandmother, Ethel Ray Nance, and her experiences allows the readers to hear not just Ethel's voice but the ability to be part of a narrative that allows for inclusion, safety, and healing.

There is such power and simplicity in speaking one's truth, especially in the context of not just trauma but healing. Being able to shift pain into possibility allows us to have hope, often when the world is on fire.

As a psychotherapist, I am grateful to be able to read about the continued importance of authenticity, healing, and the importance of speaking our voice through Karen's writings. In my private practice and working with victims of trauma, it is often the voiceless who pay the most in the culture of silence. Thank you, Karen, for allowing your grandmother's legacy, as well as your ancestor's hopes and dreams, to continue through your artistry, allowing the world to bear witness to the importance of equity, inclusion, and resilience despite pain and horror, and giving a voice to the voiceless.

There is such beauty and simplicity in speaking our truth and confronting our pain. There is power and possibility when we share our stories and uplift each other. There is a wholeness in healing and in liberation.

Thank you, Karen. You continued to do the work your ancestors were not able to finish.

In loving kindness and gratitude,
Your brother,
Francis Joseph Gallego

PREFACE

In *From Ethel Ray Nance to Kamala Harris: A Legacy of Equality and Justice*, I explore the intertwined narratives of two remarkable women: my grandmother, Ethel Ray Nance, and President Kamala Harris. Though they lived in vastly different eras-Ethel in the early 20th century and the other in the 21st century-their stories are connected by a shared commitment to equality and justice. Both women broke down barriers and championed the rights of marginalized communities, navigating complex identities in their relentless pursuit of fairness.

Ethel Ray Nance, born in 1899, emerged from a world steeped in racial discrimination and violence. Her formative years were marked by the most brutal events of racial terror in American history-the lynching of three Black men in Duluth, Minnesota, in 1920. On June 15, 1920, a mob of approximately 10,000 residents stormed the jail, forcibly removed Elias Clayton, Elmer Jackson, and Issac McGhie-three Black circus workers falsely accused of raping a white woman-and publicly lynched them just four blocks from Ethel's family home. The violence unfolded almost at their doorstep, and the proximity of the atrocity brought home the terrifying reality of life for African Americans in the United States.

The spectacle was not an isolated tragedy; it was part of a broader pattern of racial violence used to maintain white supremacy. Lynchings were more than just brutal murders-they were public displays of terror meant to reinforce the racial hierarchy and subjugate Black Americans. Such acts were intended to send a message to the entire Black community: any effort to assert equality, any attempt to challenge the status quo, could be met with deadly consequences. Despite the fear and trauma these events instilled, Ethel refused to be silenced. Instead, she transformed her grief and rage into a lifelong pursuit of justice.

Ethel's involvement in the civil rights movement reflects a fearless determination to challenge the injustices of her time. Her activism took many forms-organizing community meetings, advocating for legislation, and collaborating with fellow activists. As Minnesota's first Black stenographer in the state legislature and its first Black female police officer, she confronted the challenges of a profession dominated by white men, using her position to address issues of police violence and racial profiling. Her presence in law enforcement symbolized a challenge to the status quo, demonstrating that Black women could occupy spaces traditionally reserved for white men and use their voices to advocate for justice.

Ethel's relationships with rights leaders like Dr. W.E.B. Du Bois and Thurgood Marshall further amplified her impact. She worked closely with Du Bois and other activists, contributing to crucial discussions on race and justice. Her involvement with organizations like the NAACP and the Urban League positioned her as a vital player in the fight for civil rights, demonstrating that true change required both grassroots mobilization and strategic collaboration. Ethel's advocacy for the Dyer Anti-Lynching Bill-a landmark piece of legislation that aimed to make lynching a federal crime-was an extension of her commitment to ending racial terror.

On September 26, 1922, Dr. W.E.B. Du Bois, the editor of the NAACP magazine *The Crisis*, wrote a letter to my grandmother expressing his admiration for her work on the

Dyer Anti-Lynching Bill. The following day, on September 27, 1922, Walter White, Assistant Secretary of the NAACP, wrote her as well, acknowledging her steadfast commitment. These letters (see Appendix A & B) honored Ethel's courage and determination in pushing the Dyer Bill forward despite its ultimate failure. Her dedication inspired others within the movement, laying the groundwork for future activism and highlighting the critical need for federal intervention to address racial terror.

Unfortunately, the Dyer Bill's defeat was not an isolated event. Over the next century, more than 200 similar bills were introduced, and each time, these efforts were thwarted by the same resistance. Southern legislators, clinging to the ideology of white supremacy, blocked every proposal, using the filibuster and other procedural tactics to delay justice. Even after the civil rights movement of the 1960s, the federal government hesitated to take meaningful action against lynching. It would take 100 years—literally a full century—before anti-lynching legislation would finally be enacted with the Emmett Till Antilynching Act in 2022. This long delay starkly illustrates how deeply embedded systematic racism is in America.

The legacy of Ethel's advocacy lives on in the work of Kamala Harris. As the first Black and South Asian woman to serve as Vice President and now President of the United States, Harris represents a significant milestone in the ongoing struggle for equality. Her ascent to such a prominent position in American politics is a testament to progress and a reminder that the fight for equality remains ongoing. Harris's career has been marked by a commitment to social justice, equity, and inclusion. She has consistently advocated for policies that address systemic inequalities, dismantling barriers that disproportionately affect marginalized communities. Her work in criminal justice reform, economic equality, and healthcare access resonates deeply with the struggles Ethel faced nearly a century ago.

A key aspect of Harris's platform is her focus on criminal justice reform. As a former prosecutor, she understands the flaws within the system and has pushed for measures to promote restorative justice practices. Harris's policies also reflect an understanding of the economic disparities. She champions initiatives aimed at closing the wealth gap, expanding access to affordable housing, and ensuring equitable education for all. Her economic policies underscore the interconnectedness of social justice and economic opportunity.

As a tribute to my grandmother's legacy, I am proud to follow in her footsteps as an advocate for marginalized communities. In the early 1990s, I served as a public defender in the same county where Kamala Harris began her career as a deputy district attorney. Although we worked on opposing sides, we both represented our community, reflecting the complex dynamics of the legal system.

The legacies of Ethel Ray Nance and Kamala Harris are inseparable from the broader historical context of America's struggle for equality and justice. One significant moment in this journey was the passage of the Emmett Till Anti-Lynchings Act in 2022. Named after the young Black youth whose brutal murder in 1955 catalyzed the civil rights movement, this legislation represents a significant step toward addressing historical injustices faced by Black Americans. By making lynching a federal hate crime, the act confronts the legacy of racial terror that has haunted Black communities for generations.

On August 28, 2024, President Kamala Harris stated:

"Emmett Till was murdered in 1955. He was only 14 years old.
The story of Emmett Till and the incredible bravery of Mamie Till-Mobley helped fuel the movement for civil rights in America. We must acknowledge the horror in this part of our history and unequivocally state that lynching is and always has been a hate crime.
As a United States senator, I sponsored the Emmett Till Antilynching Act to make lynching a federal hate crime. As Vice President, I proudly stood beside our President, Joe Biden, as he signed antilynching legislation into law. As President, I will continue the fight for equality and justice."

Equally important are the efforts to preserve the memory of racial violence, exemplified by the Clayton Jackson McGhie Memorial in Duluth, Minnesota. This memorial honors the three Black men lynched in 1920, a brutal event that deeply affected Ethel and her community. It serves as a reminder of the painful history of racial violence and a symbol of resilience and resistance.

Acknowledging the past is essential for understanding the ongoing fight for justice and equality. The legacies of Ethel Ray Nance and Kamala Harris illustrate how intergenerational activism can inspire future generations. This book is not just a chronicle of their lives; it is an invitation to join the ongoing fight for a just and equitable world. In honoring their journeys, we honor the countless others who have fought for justice and equality, and we reaffirm our commitment to continue that fight in the years to come, ensuring that the progress they made will not only be preserved but also expanded for future generations.

INTRODUCTION

In *From Ethel Ray Nance to Kamala Harris: A Legacy of Equality and Justice*, we explore the interconnected legacies of two pioneering women—Ethel Ray Nance and President Kamala Harris—and their shared commitment to equality, justice, and the empowerment of marginalized communities. Although they lived in different eras, their stories are united by a common purpose: the relentless pursuit of civil rights and social justice.

Ethel's story, which began in the early 20th century, is rooted in a time of intense racial violence and systemic discrimination. She was only 21 when Ethel and her family were immeasurably impacted by the horrific lynching of Elias Clayton, Elmer Jackson, and Isaac McGhie-three young Black men accused of a crime they did not commit brutal murder just four blocks from her family home in Duluth, Minnesota. The mob's violence, witnessed by thousands of residents, was a stark reminder of the terror that Black Americans faced every day. For Ethel, this traumatic event was a turning point, solidifying her lifelong commitment to fighting for justice. With the encouragement of her father, William Henry Ray, who founded the Duluth chapter of the NAACP, Ethel took bold action in the aftermath of the lynchings. In March 1921, she persuaded Dr. W.E.B. Du Bois to travel to Duluth to speak at St. Mark's AME Church, where she gave the introductory remarks. Her determination to bring national attention to her community and rally support demonstrated her fearless resolve and burgeoning leadership.

This pivotal moment laid the foundation for Ethel's lifelong activism. She collaborated with leaders like W.E.B. Du Bois and Thurgood Marshall and worked tirelessly with organizations such as the NAACP and the Urban League to combat racial injustice. Her advocacy for the Dyer Anti-Lynching Bill—a landmark piece of legislation that sought to make lynching a federal crime—was one of her most significant contributions. Although the bill ultimately failed due to fierce resistance from Southern legislators, Ethel's efforts underscored the urgent need for federal intervention and set the stage for future activism. Her courage and persistence in the face of systemic oppression paved the way for later generations of leaders and activists, including Kamala Harris.

Kamala Harris's story, a century later, reflects the progress that civil rights pioneers like Ethel Ray Nance fought for. As the first Black and South Asian woman to serve as Vice President and now President of the United States, Harris has broken barriers and become a powerful symbol of what is possible in the ongoing fight for equality. Her rise to national leadership is the culmination of the efforts of countless advocates who came before her. Harris's career has been marked by a commitment to social justice, equity, and inclusion. As a former prosecutor, she understands the deep flaws within the criminal justice system and has worked to promote restorative justice and criminal justice reform, ensuring that those most affected by systemic inequities have a voice and a champion in positions of power.

This book not only tells the personal stories of Nance and Harris but also honors the lives and legacies of those who were denied their humanity, including Elias Clayton, Elmer Jackson, and Isaac McGhie. The Clayton Jackson McGhie Memorial in Duluth, which features statues modeled after local high school students Eddie Glen and De'Lon Grant and Dan (Pancho) Kachingwe, serves as a powerful symbol of hope and resilience. It stands as a testament to the transformative power of remembrance and the continued fight for racial justice, reminding us that the past is always present and that healing comes through acknowledgment and action.

The narrative also highlights the ongoing work of Vice President Tim Walz, the former governor of Minnesota, who has been a tireless advocate for equity and justice. On June 15, 2020, Walz commemorated the 100th anniversary of the lynchings by visiting the Clayton Jackson McGhie Memorial. He met with community members and delivered a speech outside Duluth City Hall, drawing a direct line between the lynchings of 1920 and the modern-day struggle for racial justice. His words connected the brutal murders of Clayton, Jackson, and McGhie to the killing of George Floyd in Minneapolis just weeks earlier, emphasizing that these tragedies are part of a long and painful history of racial violence in America. "This is a story of who we are," Walz said. "Without this story, without the connection to Mr. Clayton, Mr. Jackson, Mr. McGhie, and Max Mason, it's easy then not to see that there's a direct line that descends down for 100 years to George Floyd laying on the streets at 38th and Chicago."

Governor Walz's words reminded the public that racial violence and injustice are not isolated events but part of a long and continuous history. He also highlighted the significance of Max Mason's story, another young Black man wrongfully accused and convicted after the lynchings. Despite a lack of evidence, Mason was sentenced to 30 years in prison and paroled in 1925, eventually dying in Alabama at the age of 46. In 2020, the Minnesota Board of Pardons granted Mason a posthumous pardon—the first in state history. Attorney General Keith Ellison, who sits on the three-person pardon board, noted that Mason was "falsely accused and wrongly convicted," and this pardon, though symbolic, represented a long-overdue acknowledgment of the injustice he suffered.

The legacies of Ethel Ray Nance, Kamala Harris, and Tim Walz reflect the ongoing struggle for justice and equity that spans generations. By incorporating the framework of intersectionality—a concept introduced by Kimberlé Crenshaw to describe how race, gender, class, and other social identities overlap to create complex systems of discrimination and privilege—we can better understand how these leaders navigated and overcame intersecting forms of oppression. Their work continues to shape the fight for a more just and equitable society, demonstrating that the pursuit of justice is both personal and collective.

Additionally, this book sheds light on the advocacy of the Walz family for Americans with learning disabilities. The family's openness in discussing their son Gus's diagnoses of ADHD, a nonverbal learning disorder, and anxiety has helped to raise visibility and awareness. Their willingness to share their experiences offers support to other families and underscores the importance of advocacy for individuals with disabilities. This emphasis on inclusion and understanding extends the book's message of equity and justice beyond race and gender, emphasizing the need for a society that values and supports all of its members.

As we explore the stories of these leaders, let us remember that the fight for justice is ongoing and multifaceted. The narratives of Nance, Harris, and Walz remind us that progress requires resilience, courage, and a commitment to confronting injustice in all its forms. May the memories of Elias Clayton, Elmer Jackson, Isaac McGhie, and Max Mason inspire us to continue the work of those who came before, and may their legacies remind us that we must build a future where justice and equity are truly realized for all.

Chapter 1: Roots of Resilience

The story of Ethel Ray Nance's family, like so many other Black families in the late 19th and early 20th centuries, began with a relentless pursuit of safety, opportunity, and a better future. The tragic lynching of Elias Clayton, Elmer Jackson, and Isaac McGhie in 1920—just four blocks from the Ray family's home—was a horrific reminder that no place in America was truly safe for African Americans. Yet, this traumatic event served as a catalyst, not only shaping Ethel's lifelong commitment to civil rights but also highlighting the strength and resilience deeply rooted in her family's history.

Ethel's father, William Henry Ray, was a quintessential example of this resilience. His life journey, beginning in the Reconstruction-era South and culminating in the northern reaches of Minnesota, mirrored the experiences of millions of African Americans who fled the oppressive conditions of the South during the Great Migration. The Great Migration was one of the most significant demographic shifts in American history, as approximately six million Black Americans left the rural South between 1916 and 1970, seeking refuge and opportunity in Northern and Western cities. Like so many others, William Henry left his birthplace believing that the North offered a chance to escape the brutal realities of Southern racism and build a future filled with hope and possibility. But the North, as he would soon learn, had its own set of challenges and barriers to overcome.

Born in North Carolina during Reconstruction, William Henry Ray grew up in a world that was still reeling from the aftermath of the Civil War. The Reconstruction era, which lasted from 1865 to 1877, was a time of both promise and peril for newly emancipated African Americans. For the first time in U.S. history, Black men gained the right to vote and hold public office. The federal government passed the 13th, 14th, and 15th Amendments, which abolished slavery, granted citizenship, and protected voting rights. This period also saw the establishment of public schools for African Americans, the rise of Black-owned businesses, and a growing sense of autonomy and possibility.

But this progress was met with swift and violent resistance. White supremacist groups like the Ku Klux Klan rose in response, using terror, intimidation, and murder to reassert control over Black communities. African Americans were attacked, lynched, and driven out of their homes. The promise of Reconstruction gave way to the harsh realities of Jim Crow segregation, which enforced a rigid racial hierarchy and stripped African Americans of their newfound rights. For young William, growing up under these conditions meant navigating a landscape fraught with danger and uncertainty. Racial violence was not an abstract concept—it was a lived experience that shaped his worldview and fueled his desire to find a place where he could live freely and build a better life.

By the time William was 10 years old, he was orphaned and left in the care of his two older sisters. Recognizing the growing dangers for young Black men in the South, his family made the difficult decision to send him North, hoping he might find safety and opportunity there. His journey took him to Burlington, Iowa, where he was adopted by a German family—a highly unusual occurrence for the time, as most African Americans were not welcomed into white households. This adoption provided William with a rare chance to receive a formal education and develop skills that would later prove invaluable in his professional life.

As a young adult, William ventured across the Midwest, taking on a series of jobs that allowed him to witness the complex dynamics of race, labor, and opportunity in Northern cities. He worked as a porter, a factory laborer, and a delivery man, gaining firsthand experience in the growing labor movement. In Chicago, he observed the early efforts to unionize Black workers, who were often excluded from white-dominated labor unions and faced economic discrimination even in the supposedly more progressive North. In St. Louis, he witnessed the simmering racial tensions that erupted into violence in the East St. Louis Race Riots of 1917, where white mobs, enraged by the growing Black population, attacked Black neighborhoods, killing hundreds and leaving thousands homeless.

These experiences shaped William's understanding of the complexities of race and economic opportunity in America. They also instilled in him a resolve to find a place where he could build a stable life and contribute to the fight for racial justice. By 1888, he had made his way to Minneapolis, Minnesota, where he found work as a porter at the Ardmore Hotel. It was there that he met Inga Nordquist, a young Swedish immigrant who, like William, had come to Minnesota in search of a better life. Inga had left behind the rural farms of Värmland, Sweden, crossing the Atlantic with the hope that America would offer her the economic stability and opportunities that her homeland could not provide.

Their meeting was serendipitous, and despite the formidable social and racial barriers that stood between them, William and Inga fell in love. They married in 1890, creating a multiracial family in a society that viewed race in strictly binary terms. While Minnesota did not have laws against interracial marriage, their union was nonetheless seen as a direct challenge to the established racial order. Both the Black and white communities viewed interracial couples with suspicion, and William and Inga often found themselves navigating a world that did not fully embrace their relationship.

Their family grew over the next decade, each child bringing a unique personality and dynamic to the household. Their first child, William (Will) Nordquist Ray, was born in 1890. Cheerful and outgoing, he often acted as a mediator among his siblings, using humor and charm to defuse conflicts. In 1893, Ora Inga Ray was born. Ora was a quiet, passive child with a gentle disposition, much like her mother's. In 1895, the Ray family welcomed their second son, Oscar Edwin Ray. Unlike his older brother, Oscar was morose and often seemed weighed down by a sense of melancholy, reflecting a sadness that he carried with him from a young age. His introspective nature set him apart, and he sometimes struggled to find his place within the family's complex dynamic. Finally, in 1899, the youngest, Ethel May Ray, was born. Even as a child, Ethel displayed a spark of determination and curiosity, qualities that hinted at the strong-willed woman she would eventually become.

Growing up in a predominantly white neighborhood, all four children were subjected to taunts and name-calling from local children, who saw their mixed heritage as something to ridicule. The Ray boys—William and Oscar—had fairer complexions compared to their sisters, which occasionally afforded them a certain level of superficial acceptance. Ethel and Ora, however, were darker, with Ora being the darkest of the four. This, combined with Ora's quiet nature, made her an easier target for cruelty. But her father's loving words, calling her "coffee with cream," served as a powerful affirmation of her worth and beauty, countering the racist slurs she often heard.

Despite the harassment they faced outside the home, the Rays found strength within their family and sought to create a safe, nurturing environment for their children. They shielded them from the worst of society's hatred and discrimination, instilling in them a sense of dignity and pride. However, the family's sense of security was shattered in 1900 when tragedy struck. Their gentle, passive Ora, only seven years old, became gravely ill with pneumonia. In an era before the widespread availability of antibiotics, pneumonia was a serious and often fatal condition, especially for children. Nevertheless, the Rays believed they could trust the local doctor to provide proper care.

However, the doctor who treated Ora did not view the Ray family as equals. The fact that William and Inga's children were biracial meant that the doctor saw Ora's life as less valuable, her suffering as less worthy of attention. Instead of administering treatment with the care and precision expected, the doctor's casual disregard for Ora's life led him to administer a dose of medication far too strong for a small child's body to handle. Ora's condition deteriorated rapidly, and despite her parents' pleas and vigilance, she died within days. For the Ray family, the death of their beloved daughter was not just a personal tragedy—it was a cruel confirmation that racism had invaded even the sanctity of their home.

Until then, the Ray children had experienced racism primarily through the taunts and jeers of neighborhood children, the cold stares of passersby, or the exclusionary treatment at local stores and restaurants. They knew that outside their home, they were often seen as "other," but within the walls of their own house, they had believed they could protect their children from the cruelty of a prejudiced world. Ora's death shattered that illusion. It exposed a chilling reality: the hatred and discrimination they thought they could keep at bay had seeped through the cracks and taken something irreplaceable from them. The doctor's indifference and negligence were not just acts of incompetence—they were acts of violence cloaked in a thin veil of professional authority. His actions served as a reminder that racism was not always loud or overt. It could be subtle, cloaked in the decisions made by those who wielded power, and it could be just as deadly.

Ora's death marked a turning point for the Ray family. It made them acutely aware that they could not truly be safe anywhere—not even in the supposedly progressive North, not even in their own home. They realized that the very institutions meant to protect and care for their community—like healthcare—could instead be weaponized against them. The loss left deep scars on the family. It magnified Oscar's sense of hopelessness as he struggled to comprehend why his sister's life had been deemed so expendable. William Nordquist's cheerful nature dimmed, his childhood sense of security shaken. For Ethel, who was only a year old at the time, Ora's absence became an unspoken but ever-present reminder of the fragility of life and the reality of racial prejudice. Though she would never remember Ora directly, her sister's death would become part of the family narrative that shaped Ethel's understanding of the world—a world where their family's very existence was seen as a provocation.

For William Henry and Inga, the death of their daughter solidified a harsh truth: racial hatred could reach them anywhere, at any time, and in the most intimate of ways. They could not shield their children from its effects, no matter how hard they tried. The grief and anger they felt pushed them to become more vigilant, more aware of the dangers that lurked beneath the surface of their seemingly quiet Northern life. It was no longer just a matter of ensuring that their children grew up with dignity and self-respect—it was a matter of survival. The experience galvanized William's determination to fight for justice and deepened Inga's quiet resolve to stand by her husband's side, no matter the cost.

In the years that followed, the Ray family continued to face prejudice and hardship, but Ora's death remained a defining moment, shaping their approach to the world around them. William threw himself into community activism, working to establish networks of support for Black families in Duluth and speaking out against the subtle and overt forms of racism that threatened their existence. He became more involved in the local chapter of the NAACP, channeling his grief into a drive to protect other families from suffering similar tragedies. He was no longer content with merely building a safe home for his family; he wanted to ensure that Black families across the city—and eventually the country—had the protection and respect they deserved.

The legacy of Ora's short life and tragic death would ripple through the Ray family for generations. It would shape Ethel's unrelenting commitment to fighting for justice and would echo in the actions of those inspired by her work. The events of 1900 were not just a personal tragedy for one family—they were a microcosm of the larger reality faced by countless Black families across the United States. Racism could infiltrate even the safest of spaces, taking on insidious forms that left no one untouched.

Will, Oscar, and Ethel grew up in a complex and divided environment. Duluth's Black population was small, and racial divisions, while less overt than in the South, still shaped everyday life. The Ray children learned early on what it meant to be both insiders and outsiders, straddling the line between Black and white communities. This dual identity would deeply influence Ethel's sense of self and her understanding of the world.

For young Ethel, growing up in the shadow of Ora's death meant growing up with an acute awareness of the pervasiveness of racism and the precariousness of life. As she grew older, the lessons of her early childhood—of the vulnerabilities they faced even in places meant to offer refuge—would become central to her activism. She carried Ora's memory with her, transforming the trauma of her sister's death into a fierce determination to challenge the structures that allowed such injustices to occur.

Two decades after Ora's death, Ray's family's understanding of race, justice, and their place in America would be forever altered by the lynchings of 1920. The brutal murders of Elias Clayton, Elmer Jackson, and Isaac McGhie, which occurred just blocks from the Ray family's home, served as a horrific reminder that racial violence was not confined to the South—it existed in the North as well. For William and Inga, this atrocity underscored the harsh reality that no place in America was truly safe for Black families. For their daughter, Ethel, the event ignited a passion for civil rights that would define her life.

Ethel responded to the lynchings not with fear but with action. Encouraged by her father, she quickly became active in the Duluth chapter of the NAACP, organizing protests and demanding accountability for the murders. Her work brought her into contact with national civil rights leaders, including W.E.B. Du Bois, who would become a mentor and ally. Through these connections, Ethel began to envision a path forward—not just for herself but for the entire Black community.

William and Inga's courage and resilience laid the foundation for Ethel's lifelong activism. The strength they modeled in the face of adversity became a beacon of hope and determination for their daughter. Their story is not just one of personal perseverance—it is a testament to the power of resistance and the relentless pursuit of justice, even in the face of overwhelming odds.

This legacy, rooted in courage and a profound sense of justice, resonates in the life and work of Kamala Harris. The values of resilience, resistance, and unwavering commitment to equality that were passed down through generations of the Ray family continue to echo in the lives of contemporary leaders who stand on the shoulders of those who came before. Their stories, though separated by decades, are united by a shared struggle for equality and a dedication to transforming the world for future generations.

Chapter 2
The Duluth Lynchings: A Turning Point for Justice

The Ray family's understanding of racial injustice, already heightened by the tragic death of young Ora, took on new urgency on the night of June 15, 1920. That evening, a brutal act of racial violence shattered the relative quiet of Duluth, Minnesota, leaving an indelible mark on the city's history and transforming the Ray family's perception of safety and justice. Only four blocks from the Ray family's home, three young Black men—Elias Clayton, Elmer Jackson, and Isaac McGhie—were falsely accused of raping a white woman, Irene Tusken, at the John Robinson Circus, where they worked as roustabouts.

Fueled by racial hatred and a thirst for mob justice, a crowd of thousands stormed the local jail, demanding the men's release. Though the authorities initially attempted to protect the young men, the sheer size and fury of the mob overwhelmed them. Within hours, Clayton, Jackson, and McGhie were dragged from their cells, beaten, and lynched in front of a cheering crowd. The public brutality of the act, witnessed by families, children, and neighbors, was a horrific reminder that racism and racial violence could erupt anywhere—even in a Northern city that prided itself on being progressive. The gruesome spectacle exposed the depth of racial hatred lurking beneath the surface of this seemingly quiet community and shattered any illusions that the North was a refuge for Black Americans.

The lynching was not a spontaneous act of rage but a deliberate expression of white supremacy. It was meant to send a clear message to Duluth's small Black population: no matter how far north they had traveled, they were still subject to the same racial terror that characterized life in the South. For African Americans who had moved north during the Great Migration, seeking refuge from the oppressive conditions of Jim Crow, the events in Duluth were a devastating revelation. Systemic racism knew no regional boundaries-these forces permeated every corner of the nation.

For the Ray family, who had left behind the South over racism and sought to build a safe life in Duluth, this brutal event was a crushing blow. It starkly revealed that their efforts to protect their children and build a life free from racial terror had been in vain. William Henry Ray, Ethel's father, felt the lynchings as a personal failure, a painful confirmation that the systemic racism he had fled as a young man in the South was just as insidious in the North. Despite his efforts to create a safe and stable life for his family, the violence of that night made it clear that Black families could not truly be safe anywhere in America.

For Ethel, who was only 21 years old at the time, the trauma of such an atrocity so close to home had a profound and lasting impact. The violence and injustice of the lynchings crystallized her commitment to fighting for civil rights. She recognized that the struggle for justice was not limited to protecting Black lives in the South-it encompassed challenging institutional racism throughout the entire country, including places like Duluth. The tragedy transformed Ethel's understanding of her role and responsibility, propelling her to take on a more active and fearless position in the fight for racial justice.

The Duluth lynchings garnered national attention, with newspapers across the country reporting on the brutality of the event. The NAACP, under the leadership of James Weldon Johnson and W.E.B. Du Bois, immediately launched an investigation and called for federal anti-lynching legislation. The outrage over the lynchings sparked a renewed push for the Dyer Anti-Lynching Bill, which sought to make lynching a federal crime. In response, William Henry Ray founded the Duluth chapter of the NAACP, determined to channel the grief and anger into meaningful action. Together with other chapter members, including Ethel, they began organizing local campaigns, mobilizing community support, and reaching out to people of influence, urging them to write letters to Congressmen and Senators to support the legislation.

In March 1921, at her father's urging, Ethel took on a leadership role in bringing national attention to their community. With remarkable resolve, she persuaded Dr. W.E.B. Du Bois to travel to Duluth to speak at St. Mark's AME Church in support of the Dyer Anti-Lynching Bill. Standing before a packed congregation, Ethel delivered the introductory remarks, her voice steady and clear, even as the weight of what had happened in her city bore down on her. This event marked the beginning of her burgeoning leadership in the fight for civil rights, demonstrating her fearlessness and her determination to confront injustice head-on.

Although the Dyer Anti-Lynching Bill ultimately failed to pass due to opposition from Southern Democrats, the lynchings in Duluth played a key role in bringing the issue of racial violence to the forefront of national consciousness. Ethel's dedication did not go unnoticed; she received personal letters from W.E.B. Du Bois, editor of the NAACP's magazine *The Crisis*, acknowledging her tireless efforts and commitment to advancing the cause of justice. Their correspondence was a source of encouragement and served as a reminder of the importance of her work—a testament to the impact of her activism, even in the face of tremendous opposition.

The lynchings were a turning point not only for Ethel but for the broader civil rights movement. They foreshadowed the larger struggles that would unfold over the coming decades. The fight for justice, rooted in the specific atrocities of lynchings, was also about dismantling the structural racism that permeated every aspect of American life—from housing and employment to education and the criminal justice system. For Ethel, seeking justice for those who had been lynched was part of a larger mission to address the systemic inequalities that made such violence possible.

Fifty years after the lynchings, in 1979, Duluth's dark history was brought back into the spotlight by Michael Fedo, a journalist and author, whose meticulous research detailed the horrific events of that night and exposed the broader racial climate that enabled such a heinous act to occur (*The Lynchings Duluth,* Second Edition, 2016). Duluth, which had largely tried to forget the lynchings, was forced to confront its history as Fedo's book reopened the city's racial wounds and sparked renewed dialogue about its history.

In 2021, my husband and I traveled from our home in California to Minnesota, where we connected with Michael Fedo and his wife, Judith, as I worked on writing my grandmother's story and preserving my family's legacy. From our first meeting, Michael and Judith became wonderful mentors and advisors. Michael's deep understanding of Duluth's history and his work documenting the 1920 lynchings, particularly through his book, *The Lynchings in Duluth*, helped me see how deeply intertwined my grandmother's activism was with the broader history of racial justice in America.

The creation of the Clayton Jackson McGhie Memorial in Duluth was a product of decades of dedicated work by several community members who sought to honor the memory of the three Black men who were lynched in 1920. This movement gained significant momentum in 2000, during the 80th anniversary of the lynchings, when Henry Banks, a local community leader, and Heidi Bakk-Hansen, a journalist, co-founded a group that would eventually become the Clayton Jackson McGhie Memorial Board. Their efforts culminated in the completion of the memorial in 2003, featuring a striking design by local artist Carla Stetson and writer Anthony Peyton Porter. The memorial plaza includes three life-sized bronze sculptures of Elias Clayton, Elmer Jackson, and Isaac McGhie, standing with dignity and strength. Surrounded by engraved quotes from civil rights leaders, poets, and philosophers, the plaza creates a contemplative space for visitors to reflect on the tragedy and its ongoing significance. This memorial stands not only as a tribute to the three victims but also as a call to remember, confront, and learn from the dark chapters of history.

Since its dedication, the Clayton Jackson McGhie Memorial has become a focal point for annual commemorations, educational initiatives, and public discussions. The memorial now serves as more than a historical marker—it is a powerful symbol of the community's ongoing commitment to truth, reconciliation, and racial justice. It provides a space for healing and remembrance and has become a vital part of Duluth's identity, reminding residents and visitors alike of the importance of confronting past injustices.

For me, as the granddaughter of Ethel Ray Nance, the memorial is a powerful reminder of why my grandmother's work in civil rights was so important. Her activism, born out of the trauma of the Duluth lynchings, left an indelible mark on the fight for justice and equality. The work she began in Duluth would continue through the generations, reminding all of us that the pursuit of justice requires us to confront painful truths about our past.

The connection between the Duluth lynchings and the modern fight for justice is clear. The same issues of systemic racism, police brutality, and racial violence that Ethel fought against remain central to the civil rights movement today. Kamala Harris, as President of the United States, carries forward the legacy of activists like Ethel Ray Nance, using her platform to address these deeply rooted injustices. Harris's sponsorship of the Emmett Till Anti-Lynching Act is a direct continuation of the work that Ethel began nearly a century ago. The passage of this landmark legislation is a testament to the persistence and resilience of those who have fought for justice in the face of overwhelming odds.

The journey toward racial equality is far from over, but the work of individuals like Ethel and Kamala Harris serves as a testament to the power of advocacy and the possibility of progress, even in the face of the most daunting challenges. Their stories remind us that while progress is often hard-won, the fight for justice must continue, building on the legacy of those who came before us to create a more equitable future for all.

This commitment to justice and equity is also reflected in the Clayton Jackson McGhie Memorial, which stands at the site of the lynching as a reminder of the need for accountability and healing. The memorial's use of local high school students—Eddie Glen, Dan (Pancho) Kachingwe, and De'Lon Grant—as models for the statues of Clayton,

Jackson, and McGhie brings this legacy into the present, bridging the gap between the past and the future.

Glen, Kachingwe, and Grant have each gone on to build remarkable careers that embody the potential that was cruelly denied to the victims of the lynching. Eddie Glen, now a software engineer and public defender, advocates for justice by leveraging his expertise in technology and law. Dan "Pancho" Kachingwe, a successful restaurant owner in California, has channeled his entrepreneurial spirit into creating a community-focused business that celebrates diversity and resilience. De'Lon Grant, a multi-hyphenate creative, has dedicated his life to fostering inclusive creative spaces and diverse storytelling as a theater artist, photographer, and educator.

The Clayton Jackson McGhie Memorial stands as a powerful testament to the transformation of racial trauma into a legacy of justice and remembrance. The stories of Glen, Kachingwe, and Grant—intertwined with the legacy of Ethel Ray Nance and the continued work of Kamala Harris—remind us that the fight for justice is ongoing but that each step forward builds on the sacrifices and struggles of those who came before us. Progress is not linear, and setbacks are inevitable, but the work of individuals like Ethel, Kamala, and these young role models—21 years later—demonstrates that change is always possible, even in the face of the most entrenched injustice. Their successes, in many ways, are living tributes to the dreams and potential of Clayton, Jackson, and McGhie.

Chapter 3
Navigating Identity:

The Ray Children and the Burden of Passing

The story of the Ray children—my grandmother Ethel and her brothers, Will and Oscar—is a profound exploration of the complexities of racial identity in early 20th-century America. As the offspring of William Henry Ray, a Black man who had migrated north from North Carolina, and Inga Nordquist, a Swedish immigrant, they grew up in a family that defied the rigid racial boundaries of their time. The Ray children lived at the intersection of two worlds—one defined by the legacy of American slavery and racial violence and the other shaped by the immigrant experience and the hope of a better life. This unique position placed them in a constant struggle between identity and survival as they navigated a society that demanded conformity to a strict binary understanding of race. Each sibling faced the heavy burden of figuring out where they belonged in a racially divided America, a task that came with severe emotional and psychological costs.

The lynchings of Elias Clayton, Elmer Jackson, and Isaac McGhie in Duluth, which had such a powerful impact on Ethel's sense of purpose, also reverberated deeply within her brothers. Each of the Ray siblings would process these events differently, shaping the paths they chose in response to the racial violence that occurred mere blocks from their home. The trauma of that night, coupled with their already fraught experience of growing up biracial in a deeply segregated society, left an indelible mark on each of their lives. For Will, Oscar, and Ethel, the question of identity was not merely a personal dilemma-it was a matter of survival.

In many ways, the Ray children's experiences illustrate the emotional toll of being multiracial in a society that refused to acknowledge the complexity of mixed-race identities. They were forced to learn early on that their racial identity could not be easily categorized, leaving them vulnerable to discrimination from both Black and white communities. As a result, each sibling chose a different path to survive the complexities of race in America. Their divergent choices not only shaped their personal lives but also reflected the deeply ingrained racism that permeated American society—a society that struggled to reconcile its professed ideals of freedom and equality with its oppressive reality.

For Will Ray, the eldest son, the pressures of living as a Black man in a racially segregated society became overwhelming. Though his complexion was lighter than his father's, and he could pass as white, Will's early experiences with racism left deep scars. From a young age, he understood that his skin color would dictate his opportunities, no matter his talents or ambitions. Even in the supposedly more tolerant North, the reality was that racial prejudice was often just as insidious and covert as in the South. By the time Will was 18, the weight of these limitations had become too much to bear. He made the difficult decision to leave Duluth and move to Portland, Oregon, where he began living as a white man.

Passing as white allowed Will to escape the immediate dangers and limitations imposed on Black men, but it also required him to sever ties with his family and his Black heritage. For Will, passing was not just a matter of survival—it was a way to access opportunities that would otherwise have been denied to him. The emotional cost of living a lie, however, weighed heavily on him. Passing meant constantly living in fear of being exposed, knowing that his true identity could cost him everything he had built in his new life. He navigated a precarious existence, where one slip of the tongue or a chance encounter with someone from his past could unravel the carefully constructed identity he had assumed. The fear of discovery and the isolation that came with it created a sense of estrangement that would follow him for the rest of his life.

Will's decision to pass as white was not unique. Many African Americans during this time chose to pass to escape the harsh realities of racial discrimination. The phenomenon of passing reflected the rigid racial hierarchy that defined American society. For those who could pass, the decision was often seen as a means of survival, but it also came with significant emotional and psychological consequences. Passing required individuals to deny their true selves, to live in constant fear of being found out, and to cut themselves off from their families and communities. The cost of passing was not just the loss of familial connections but also a profound sense of disconnection from oneself. Will's story, like those of many who passed, is a tragic reminder of the lengths to which African Americans had to go to navigate a society that valued whiteness above all else.

Oscar Ray, the middle child, took a different path. While Will fully embraced passing as a means of escaping racial discrimination, Oscar chose to remain in Duluth but lived a dual existence—identifying as a white man with people who did not know his family and as a Black man with those who did. This dual identity allowed Oscar to navigate a broader social world, but it came with its own set of challenges. To outsiders unaware of his family background, Oscar was a white man who fit comfortably within white society. Yet, when he was with his family or in Black social circles, he was seen as a Black man. Living with this dual identity required constant vigilance, and the fear of being "found out" haunted him.

The psychological strain of living between two worlds—one Black and one white—took a toll on Oscar's mental health. He often found himself caught between conflicting desires: the desire for acceptance in white society and the desire to stay true to his heritage and familial ties. This internal conflict left him struggling to find his place in a society that offered no space for the complexity of his existence. Though he did not face the complete severing of ties that Will experienced, Oscar's position was equally precarious. Passing selectively required him to compartmentalize his life in a way that deepened his sense of dislocation and loneliness.

Oscar's internal conflict came to a head on the night of June 15, 1920—the night of the Duluth lynchings. As the mob gathered outside the jail, Oscar found himself caught up in the frenzy. Though he did not participate in the violence, he was swept along with the crowd, shouting as Elias Clayton, Elmer Jackson, and Isaac McGhie were dragged from their cells and hanged. The experience forced Oscar to confront his own identity in ways he had never before imagined. He knew that in the eyes of the mob, he was just as vulnerable as Clayton, Jackson, and McGhie. Yet, because he could pass as white, he was granted a kind of safety that his Black peers were denied.

For Oscar, the lynchings were a moment of reckoning. He wrestled with the moral implications of passing and the privileges it afforded him. The psychological strain of living with this internal conflict would haunt Oscar for the rest of his life. He struggled to reconcile his desire for the privileges of whiteness with his connection to his Black roots. His decision to remain in Duluth, rather than follow Will's path of complete passing, was an attempt to hold on to his identity, but it came at a significant emotional cost. The events of that night served as a constant reminder of the tenuous nature of his existence and the societal forces that sought to tear him apart. For Oscar, choosing to live in both worlds was a form of resistance, but it was also a choice that came with its own burdens.

For my grandmother, Ethel Ray Nance, the events of 1920 had the opposite effect. Rather than retreating from her Black identity, Ethel embraced it fully. From an early age, she had been her father's confidante, learning from him about the importance of standing up for what was right and advocating for justice. The lynchings of Clayton, Jackson, and McGhie served as a catalyst for Ethel's activism, pushing her to the forefront of the fight for civil rights. While her brothers struggled with the burdens of passing, Ethel took pride in her Black heritage and saw it as a source of strength.

Ethel channeled her anger and frustration into activism, working closely with the NAACP and civil rights leaders like W.E.B. Du Bois and Thurgood Marshall. She believed that true justice could only be achieved by confronting the systems of oppression that had allowed racial violence and discrimination to persist for so long. Ethel's commitment to justice was not just about seeking retribution for the lynchings—it was about addressing the deeper, systemic issues that underpin racial inequality in America. She understood that passing, while a means of escaping immediate discrimination, was not a solution to the larger problem of white supremacy. Instead, Ethel chose to fight for a society in which Black men and women could live freely and openly without fear of violence or discrimination.

The story of the Ray children reflects the broader challenges faced by African Americans during the early 20th century. Their experiences with racial identity and passing illustrate the emotional and psychological burdens imposed by a society that rigidly enforced racial boundaries. Will's decision to pass allowed him to escape some of the limitations imposed on Black men, but it came at the cost of his connection to his family and his true identity. Oscar's struggle to balance his desire for the privileges of whiteness with his connection to his Black roots left him in a state of constant tension. Ethel's choice to fully embrace her Blackness and fight for justice set her apart from her brothers and placed her at the forefront of the civil rights movement.

The burden of passing was not just about escaping racial discrimination; it was also about the psychological toll of denying one's true identity in order to survive in a society that placed immense value on whiteness. Ethel's legacy serves as a reminder of the power of resilience and the importance of embracing one's identity, even in the face of overwhelming odds. Her commitment to justice and equality laid the groundwork for future generations of civil rights leaders, including Kamala Harris, whose rise to national prominence as the first Black and South Asian woman to serve as Vice President and now President of the United States is a testament to the enduring power of resistance and resilience.

The experiences of the Ray children reflect the broader narrative of race and identity in America. Their stories remind us that the struggle for equality is not just about laws and policies—it is also about the deeply personal decisions that individuals must make in the face of a society that constantly seeks to define and limit them. The burden of passing, the weight of racial discrimination, and the resilience of those who choose to fight for a better future are themes that continue to resonate today in the fight for justice and equality.

Chapter 4: A Turning Point in Activism

Ethel Ray Nance's journey as an activist truly began to take form in the aftermath of the Duluth lynchings, but her work extended far beyond that singular, tragic event. The lynchings were a personal catalyst, transforming her anger and grief into a relentless pursuit of justice. They also served as a stark reminder that the fight for racial equality required more than isolated acts of resistance-it demanded organized and sustained efforts that could challenge the entrenched systems of oppression in America. Building on her family's legacy of resilience, Ethel became deeply engaged in the broader civil rights movements of her time, emerging as a key figure who bridged the gap between grassroots activism and cultural advocacy. Her work not only reflects the evolution of activism during the first half of the 20th century but also underscores how her multifaceted approach was essential in connecting local struggles to the national civil rights agenda.

One of the defining aspects of Ethel's activism was her ability to serve as a bridge between grassroots organizing and the broader cultural movements that were gaining momentum in the 1920s and 1930s. The Harlem Renaissance—a vibrant response to the racial injustices that African Americans faced across the country—was one such movement that Ethel engaged with, both personal and professional. As a close collaborator with W.E.B. Du Bois, a central figure of the Harlem Renaissance, she contributed to elevating the voices of Black writers, artists, and intellectuals who were using their talents to advocate for social change.

One of Ethel's most significant contributions to the Harlem Renaissance was her role in organizing the *Opportunity* Literary Dinner in New York City in 1924. This landmark event brought some of the most influential Black artists, writers, and thinkers of the time, including Langston Hughes, Zora Neale Hurston, and Claude McKay. The dinner was a celebration of Black literary achievement, but it was also a strategic gathering designed to foster collaboration and solidarity among the attendees. The *Opportunity* Dinner helped cement the importance of cultural production as a tool for advancing civil rights and underscored the idea that art and activism were deeply intertwined. By bringing these creative minds together, Ethel helped create a space where Black intellectuals could challenge dominant narratives and assert their visions of what a just society should look like.

Ethel's involvement with *Opportunity* magazine, where she worked as Charles S. Johnson's assistant, exemplified her belief in the power of cultural advocacy. *Opportunity* was more than just a literary magazine—it was a platform for intellectual discourse on issues of race, justice, and social progress. Through her contributions to the magazine and her involvement in its events, Ethel helped to create a space where Black voices could be amplified, where ideas could be debated, and where strategies for social change could be developed. She believed that by elevating the voices of Black artists and thinkers, she was not only contributing to the cultural vitality of her community but also advancing the broader civil rights agenda.

In addition to her cultural work, Ethel was also deeply involved in grassroots organizing and community building. Her work at the Phyllis Wheatley Settlement House in Minneapolis was a testament to her commitment to empowering local communities. Named after the famed Black poet Phyllis Wheatley, the settlement house served as a vital resource for Black families in Minneapolis, providing educational programs, vocational training, and social services. Ethel's role at the settlement house was multifaceted—she organized events, coordinated programs, and worked closely with families to address their needs.

The settlement house movement, which began in the late 19th century, was originally focused on addressing the needs of European immigrants in urban areas. By the time Ethel became involved, the movement had expanded to include African American communities, many of whom were facing the challenges of segregation, poverty, and limited access to education and employment. Ethel's work at the Phyllis Wheatley House reflected her belief that social justice required not only political advocacy but also direct support for individuals and families who were struggling to survive in a deeply unequal society.

Ethel's activism extended beyond the local level as well. Her involvement with the National Association for the Advancement of Colored People (NAACP) was one of the defining aspects of her career. Founded in 1909, the NAACP was the leading civil rights organization in the country, focusing on challenging racial segregation and discrimination through legal action, public education, and grassroots organizing. Ethel's work with the NAACP began in Minnesota, but it quickly expanded to the national stage as her leadership and commitment to justice grew.

One of the most notable examples of Ethel's national advocacy was her involvement in the fight for anti-lynching legislation. In the years following the Duluth lynchings, Ethel became increasingly committed to the passage of federal laws that would hold perpetrators of lynching accountable and prevent such acts of racial terror from continuing unchecked. The Dyer Anti-Lynching Bill, which was first introduced in Congress in 1918, was one of the NAACP's top legislative priorities during this period. Although the bill ultimately failed to pass due to the opposition of Southern Democrats, Ethel's advocacy for anti-lynching laws helped to raise awareness about the urgency of the issue.

In 1945, Ethel's relationship with Du Bois would bring her to another historic moment. As the world emerged from the devastation of World War II, the United Nations was founded in San Francisco with the aim of preventing future conflicts and fostering international cooperation. W.E.B. Du Bois, serving as the NAAP Consultant to the American Delegation, was determined to ensure that issues of racial discrimination and colonialism were included in the global conversation. Recognizing Ethel's dedication and capabilities, he asked her to serve as his secretary and research assistant at the founding of the United Nations. This role placed Ethel at the center of a critical moment in history, allowing her to contribute directly to discussions about human rights and global justice.

Her participation at the United Nations reflected the broadening scope of her activism—from local and national issues to the global stage. It was a testament to her ability to navigate complex social and political landscapes and to amplify the voices of marginalized communities wherever she went. Ethel's involvement with the United Nations, alongside Du Bois, underscored her belief that the fight for civil rights was not confined to American soil but was part of a larger global struggle for human dignity and equality.

Ethel was a dedicated member of the California Bay Area NAACP-GI Assistance Committee, which, in 1951, raised over $5,000 to support NAACP special counsel Thurgood Marshall, who was investigating charges of widespread court-martials of Black servicemen in Tokyo, Japan. Ethel Ray Nance was a dedicated member of this committee, contributing to the efforts to address the injustices faced by African American military personnel. Her work with the NAACP also connected her with some of the most influential figures of the civil rights movement. In addition to her close relationship with W.E.B. Du Bois, she collaborated with leaders like James Weldon Johnson, who served as the NAACP's executive secretary.

Marshall, serving as legal counsel for the NAACP, fought tirelessly for the equality of African Americans in various contexts, using his legal acumen to challenge systemic racism in the courts. His commitment culminated in the landmark Brown v. Board of Education case in 1954, where he successfully argued that racial segregation in public schools was unconstitutional. This pivotal Supreme Court ruling not only ended segregation in education but also marked a significant victory in the broader civil rights movement.

On October 2, 1967, Thurgood Marshall made history by becoming the first African American Supreme Court Justice. His appointment signified a monumental step toward greater representation and justice within the highest court in the land, furthering his lifelong mission to ensure equality and civil rights for all Americans. Through her involvement with the NAACP, Ethel Ray Nance played a vital role in this transformative era, working alongside Marshall and other prominent leaders to advance the cause of civil rights.

Ethel's activism was not limited to racial justice alone. She also advocated for women's rights, recognizing that the fight for gender equality was deeply connected to the fight for racial equality. She was a strong supporter of women's suffrage and worked to ensure that Black women were included in the broader women's rights movement. Ethel understood that Black women faced a unique set of challenges often overlooked by white feminists, and she used her platform to advocate for the rights and needs of Black women in particular.

The breadth of Ethel Ray Nance's activism—from cultural advocacy to grassroots organizing to national and international civil rights leadership—reflects the multifaceted nature of the fight for justice. Her ability to move between different spheres of influence and her commitment to addressing the interconnected issues of race, gender, and economic inequality made her a powerful force for change. Ethel's legacy as an activist is not only defined by the events she participated in or the organizations she worked with but also by the countless lives she touched through her dedication to justice.

Ethel Ray Nance's work laid the foundation for future generations of activists, including Kamala Harris, whose rise to political prominence would have been unthinkable without the groundwork laid by women like Ethel. Harris, like Ethel, understood the importance of bridging the gap between cultural representation and political power. As the first Black and South Asian woman to serve as Vice President and later President of the United States, Harris's achievements reflect the enduring legacy of Ethel's commitment to justice and equality. Ethel's belief in the power of culture and community to drive social change is a belief that continues to shape the fight for justice today.

Chapter 5

The Emmett Till Anti-Lynching Act: A Long-Awaited Victory

On March 29, 2022, history was made when President Joe Biden signed into law the Emmett Till Anti-Lynching Act, a piece of legislation that had been over a century in the making. For civil rights activists, lawmakers, and the families of lynching victims, this was a moment of both triumph and reflection—a long overdue acknowledgment of the countless Black lives lost to racial terror in the United States. The act's passage was not just a legal victory but a culmination of decades of activism, advocacy, and struggle that spanned generations.

The legislation is named after Emmett Till, a 14-year-old Black boy whose brutal murder in Mississippi in 1955 shocked the nation and galvanized the civil rights movement. Falsely accused of whistling at a white woman. Till was kidnapped, tortured, and lynched by two white men who were later acquitted by an all-white jury. Till's mother, Mamie Till-Mobley, insisted on an open casket at his funeral to show the world the horrific violence inflicted on her son. Images of Till's mutilated body circulated widely, becoming a rallying cry for civil rights activists and exposing the brutal realities of racial violence.

Till's murder was part of a larger pattern of racial terror that plagued Black communities for generations. Between 1882 and 1968, over 4,700 lynchings were recorded in the United States, most of them targeting Black men and women. These acts of violence were not isolated; they were part of a systemic effort to maintain white supremacy and prevent Black Americans from achieving social, political, and economic equality. Lynching was a public spectacle meant to send a clear message: any assertion of Black rights would be met with deadly consequences.

The fight for anti-lynching legislation was fraught with opposition. Since the early 20th century, activists like Ethel Ray Nance and organizations such as the NAACP tirelessly advocated for federal anti-lynching laws. The first major effort came in 1918 with the introduction of the Dyer Anti-Lynching Bill, named after Congressman Leonidas Dyer of Missouri. Though the bill passed the House of Representatives in 1922, it was blocked by Southern Democrats in the Senate. Despite overwhelming evidence of the brutality of lynching, the federal government framed it as a "states' rights" issue, and Southern lawmakers, intent on upholding the racial hierarchy, resisted any federal intervention.

For Ethel Ray Nance and her fellow activists, the failure of the Dyer Bill was a painful reminder of the limitations of the legal system in addressing racial violence. However, they did not give up. They continued to push for anti-lynching laws, even as the number of lynchings began to decline in the mid-20th century. Their efforts were not just about passing legislation; they sought to hold the country accountable for the atrocities committed against Black people and create a legal framework to prevent such violence in the future.

The long road to the Emmett Till Anti-Lynching Act's passage was marked by both progress and setbacks. In 2005, the U.S. Senate issued a formal apology for its failure to pass anti-lynching laws, acknowledging how federal inaction allowed racial violence to continue unchecked. But activists demanded more than an apology; they wanted real protections. This push gained momentum in 2018 when the Senate passed the Justice for Victims of Lynching Act, co-sponsored by Senators Kamala Harris, Cory Booker, and Tim Scott. However, despite its symbolic importance, it failed to pass in the House.

The turning point came in 2020, amid nationwide protests following the murder of George Floyd. With heightened awareness of systemic racism, the Emmett Till Anti-Lynching Act was reintroduced and passed with overwhelming bipartisan support. The act makes lynching a federal hate crime punishable by up to 30 years in prison, sending a powerful message about the country's commitment to addressing the legacy of racial violence. When President Biden signed the bill into law in 2022, Vice President Kamala Harris stood by his side, symbolizing the progress made and the work that still lies ahead.

For Kamala Harris, the passage of the Emmett Till Anti-Lynching Act was deeply personal. Throughout her career as a prosecutor, California Attorney General, and U.S. Senator, she worked to address racial violence and hate crimes. Her sponsorship of the bill was a continuation of the advocacy work begun by figures like Ethel Ray Nance nearly a century earlier. Harris recognized that achieving justice extends beyond legislation—it requires transforming the societal attitudes that have long devalued Black lives and creating a legal framework that ensures accountability for acts of racial terror.

The Emmett Till Anti-Lynching Act stands as both a legal and symbolic victory. It acknowledges the pain and suffering of the past while also providing a pathway for accountability in the future. Ethel Ray Nance's legacy is intricately connected to the passage of this historic law. Her work with the NAACP and her advocacy for anti-lynching legislation laid the foundation for the progress realized in 2022. This act is not just a victory for those who fought for justice in the past—it is a testament to the enduring power of activism and the importance of continuing the fight for racial equality.

However, the passage of this law is a reminder that the fight for justice is never truly over. While lynching may no longer be as common as it once was, racial violence in other forms continues to plague our society. The murder of George Floyd in 2020, just months before the Emmett Till Anti-Lynching Act was reintroduced, is a stark reminder of the ongoing struggle against systemic racism and police brutality. Floyd's death, like Till's, was more than just a tragic loss of life—it was a powerful catalyst for change, sparking global protests and renewed demands for accountability and reform. The emotional resonance of Floyd's murder, juxtaposed with the signing of the Emmett Till Act, underscores the reality that while legislative victories are critical, they are not enough to eradicate the deep-seated racism that still permeates American society.

The passage of the Emmett Till Anti-Lynching Act was a significant step forward, but it was not the final chapter in the quest for justice. As long as racial violence in any form continues to exist, the fight for justice must continue. The law is a crucial tool, but true justice requires a sustained commitment to confronting the root causes of racial hatred and inequality. The legacies of Ethel Ray Nance, Kamala Harris, and the many others who fought for this legislation serve as a powerful reminder that real change is possible when individuals and communities come together to demand it. Their stories are a testament to the power of collective action and the importance of honoring the work of those who came before us by continuing to fight for a more just and equitable future.

The intertwining narratives of Ethel Ray Nance, Kamala Harris, and the Emmett Till Anti-Lynching Act highlight a broader narrative. This legislative victory is a step toward a more just society, but it is crucial to honor the legacies of those who fought before us and to carry forward their work in the ongoing pursuit of justice for all.

Chapter 6
Connecting Legacies: Ethel Ray Nance's Minnesota-California Bridge and Kamala Harris's Return

As the Emmett Till Anti-Lynching Act became law, it symbolized not only a long-overdue victory for civil rights advocates but also the continued impact of historical legacies on modern movements. This progress reflects the enduring influence of trailblazers like Ethel Ray Nance, whose fight for racial justice laid the groundwork for today's victories. Her legacy, intertwined with the leadership of President Kamala Harris and Vice President Tim Walz, demonstrates how the struggles and triumphs of past generations shape current efforts to build a more just society.

Ethel Ray Nance's story began in Minnesota—a state often seen as progressive, yet one that has long grappled with racial and social disparities. It was here, nearly a century after Ethel's pioneering work as the first Black stenographer in the Minnesota House of Representatives, that Tim Walz emerged as a dedicated advocate for racial equity and inclusion. The Harris-Walz presidency is a living testament to Ethel's influence, aligning directly with the spaces and causes she championed throughout her life. As governor, Walz's leadership focused on expanding equity and justice for marginalized communities, echoing the same spirit of advocacy that drove Ethel's work.

One of Walz's notable efforts in Minnesota was establishing the Minnesota Office of Missing and Murdered Indigenous Relatives in 2021, addressing the longstanding crisis of violence against Native American women. This initiative reflects Walz's commitment to making sure the state recognizes and addresses injustices against historically marginalized communities—something Ethel would have supported wholeheartedly. The creation of this office stands as a continuation of the fight for justice. Ethel began nearly a century earlier.

Minnesota's racial history came full circle during Walz's visit to the Clayton Jackson McGhie Memorial in Duluth on the 100th anniversary of the 1920 lynchings of Elias Clayton, Elmer Jackson, and Isaac McGhie. This tragedy, which occurred just blocks from Ethel's childhood home, had a profound impact on her life and sparked her commitment to civil rights. Walz's presence at the memorial, just weeks after George Floyd's murder, underscored the connection between the past and present racial violence and the importance of acknowledging Minnesota's painful history to pave the way to healing and change.

Walz's efforts to confront Minnesota's legacy of racial violence extend beyond symbolic gestures. His administration prioritized economic opportunities, expanded healthcare access, and promoted policies that support low-income families and people of color, reflecting Ethel's own dedication to addressing systemic inequalities. This work laid the foundation for Peggy Flanagan, who served as Walz's lieutenant governor before becoming Minnesota's first female governor and the nation's first female Native American governor. Flanagan's rise symbolizes the ongoing expansion of representation that Ethel fought for, highlighting the progress made in creating a more inclusive political landscape.

But Ethel's influence reaches far beyond Minnesota. In 1945, her journey led her and her family to San Francisco, where she served as W.E.B. Du Bois's secretary and research assistant at the founding of the United Nations. Her work with Du Bois placed her at the center of a pivotal moment in history, bridging the local activism she began in Minnesota with a broader international focus on human rights. This move also created a bridge between two significant civil rights hubs: Minnesota and California.

San Francisco would become a key location for Ethel's descendants, including her granddaughter Karen Nance. Karen, a Bay Area attorney, continued the family's legacy by serving the same community where Kamala Harris launched her groundbreaking career as the first female, African American, and South Asian District Attorney of San Francisco. This intergenerational legacy, which began in Minnesota and extended to California, connects two eras of civil rights leadership and highlights the enduring impact of Ethel's work.

In April 2024, I honored my grandmother's legacy by publishing *Ethel Ray: Living in the White, Gray, and Black*. Released on April 13th—what would have been Ethel's 125th birthday—the book celebrates her extraordinary contributions to social justice. Thanks to the efforts of Henry Banks, a Duluth community activist and member of the Duluth School Board, April 13th is now officially recognized as Ethel Ray Nance Day in Duluth. Established on April 13, 2023, Ethel Ray Nance Day serves as a powerful tribute to a woman who dedicated her life to fighting for racial equality and ensures that her legacy will continue to inspire future generations.

The Harris-Walz presidency is, in many ways, the realization of Ethel's dreams and aspirations. It stands as a testament to the progress that has been made, even as it acknowledges the work that still needs to be done. The administration's focus on addressing systemic racism, promoting reproductive rights, supporting the LGBTQ+ community, and advancing Native American sovereignty echoes Ethel's vision of a world where justice is not confined to one group but is accessible to all. Ethel's understanding of the intersectionality of race, gender, and economic inequality was revolutionary for her time, and today's leaders are carrying forward her fight, ensuring that historically marginalized voices are not just included but centered in decision-making processes.

Ethel's legacy reminds us that change is often incremental and generational and that the seeds of progress planted by one generation can blossom into transformative movements for the next. The Harris-Walz administration, with its commitment to equity and justice, stands as a living embodiment of Ethel's life and the values she championed. From the state of Minnesota, where Ethel first broke barriers, to the national and international stages, where she continued her work for justice, their leadership is a celebration of her enduring influence.

As we move forward in the ongoing fight for justice and equity, Ethel Ray Nance's legacy serves as a guiding light, reminding us that the work is never truly finished. It is an intergenerational journey that requires courage, vision, and the resilience to continue pushing boundaries. The Harris-Walz presidency, much like Ethel's own life, is a testament to the power of persistence, the importance of representation, and the necessity of honoring those who came before us by carrying their work forward into the future.

Chapter 7
Bridging Legacies & Intersectionality Justice Across Generations

The fight for equality and justice is not just about individual achievements or isolated moments in history—it's about how the efforts and sacrifices of one generation influence and shape the next. Ethel Ray Nance's legacy has flowed through time, impacting the work of contemporary leaders like President Kamala Harris and my own journey as a lawyer and advocate. Her fight for justice laid the foundation for a continuum of advocacy, where each generation adds its own light to illuminate the path forward. This continuum now extends through my podcast, *Connecting with Karen Nance*, where we can explore these intersecting legacies and create a platform for new voices to push the boundaries of what justice can look like.

The Harris-Walz presidency is a living testament to Ethel's influence, symbolizing the completion of a "Minnesota-California bridge" that Ethel began, stretching from her groundbreaking activism in Minnesota's political sphere to her move to San Francisco to work alongside W.E.B. Du Bois. Their collaborative efforts have expanded this bridge, connecting the ideas Ethel championed-justice, inclusivity, and equity—with Kamala Harris' historic role as the first African American and Asian American Vice President, and now President, and Tim Walz's ongoing commitment as her Vice President.

Ethel's work was trailblazing in every sense of the word. As a civil rights activist, cultural advocate, and community organizer, she laid the groundwork for much of today's progress. Her activism was not limited to one issue or community; she believed in the interconnectedness of all struggles for equality—whether they focused on race, gender, or economic inequality. This comprehensive approach to justice is central to understanding the concept of intersectionality—a term not formally defined until Kimberlé Crenshaw introduced it in the late 1980s but one that Ethel practiced intuitively.

Her work with the NAACP, *Opportunity* magazine, and the Phyllis Wheatley Settlement House reflected her commitment to addressing the multiple, overlapping forms of oppression that African Americans—particularly Black women—faced. As the first Black stenographer in the Minnesota House of Representatives, Ethel defied societal expectations and helped pave the way for future generations. Her efforts were not confined to breaking barriers for herself but focused on ensuring others could follow.

This legacy of intersectionality and advocacy continues to influence my own career choices. Inspired by Ethel's belief that the law can be a tool for justice, I became a lawyer. My role as a public defender and Kamala's role as a district attorney were distinct, yet both played essential roles in ensuring the fair administration of justice. As a restorative justice facilitator in the California Department of Corrections, I have seen firsthand the transformative power of healing through dialogue and reconciliation—a philosophy deeply rooted in the idea of addressing systematic injustice rather than merely punishing individuals. This work is a direct continuation of my grandmother's belief in community empowerment and her commitment to addressing the root causes of inequality.

Beyond the confines of the legal system, my podcast, *Connecting with Karen Nance*, serves as a modern platform to honor Ethel's legacy and amplify the voices of those building their own legacies of justice and equity. Each guest brings unique perspectives, but they are all united by their commitment to creating a more inclusive and just society. Whether through environmental advocacy, educational reform, or healthcare equity, their work underscores that the fight for justice is not confined to any one issue or profession—it is a collective effort that requires each of us to contribute.

Intersectionality has always been at the heart of Ethel's activism. While the term itself may be new, the understanding that struggles for justice are interconnected is not. As a Black woman working in the early 20th century, Ethel recognized that the racism she faced was compounded by the sexism she encountered, shaping both her daily experiences and her activism. This intersectional awareness drove her to address issues affecting Black men and women alike, to fight for the dignity of workers, and to include marginalized voices in every sphere of society.

Kamala Harris's presidency is a powerful testament to the importance of intersectionality in leadership and governance. As the first woman, the first Black woman, and the first South Asian woman to hold the office of President of the United States, Harris embodies the multiplicity of experiences that intersectionality seeks to address. Her rise to the highest office is not just a victory for one group—it is a victory for many marginalized communities that see themselves reflected in her leadership. Her work on criminal justice reform, environmental policy, and healthcare equity reflects her understanding of the need to address overlapping systems of oppression.

The stories of my podcast guests serve as a reminder that intersectionality is not just an academic concept—it is a lived reality that shapes the experiences of individuals and communities every day. From the intersection of race and disability to environmental justice and economic inequality, my guests highlight how understanding these overlaps is crucial to achieving meaningful change. Leaders like Harris, activists like Ethel Ray Nance, and everyday advocates are pushing us to engage with the full complexity of the issues at hand.

The ongoing legacy of justice and equity began with individuals like my grandmother and continues through people like Kamala Harris and the many guests featured on *Connecting with Karen Nance*. Creating a legacy of justice is not just a professional calling; it's a deeply personal commitment. As I navigate my role as an advocate and ally, I am constantly inspired by the stories of those around me and the enduring impact of my grandmother's life.

As we move forward in our collective fight for justice, the lessons of intersectionality offer a roadmap for how to build more inclusive movements, policies, and communities. The Harris-Walz leadership, much like Ethel's own life, reminds us that change is often incremental and generational and that the seeds of progress planted by one generation can blossom into transformative movements for the next. Their leadership is a celebration of Ethel's enduring influence—a testament that the fight for justice is never truly over but rather an ongoing journey that requires courage, vision, and resilience from all who dare to dream of a more equitable world.

The future of justice is intersectional. As more people come to understand this, we will be better equipped to create a world where everyone, regardless of race, gender, class, or other identities, can live with dignity and opportunity. Intersectionality moves us forward by reminding us that our struggles are interconnected and that together, we can build a more just and equitable future.

Chapter 8. Modern Trailblazers: Continuing the Legacy for Justice and Intersectionality

The individuals featured in this chapter embody the principles of advocacy, equity, and intersectionality that define the legacies of Ethel Ray Nance and Kamala Harris. Through their unique contributions, they carry forward the fight for a more inclusive and equitable world, addressing complex social, cultural, and economic issues. In the spirit of Ethel's pioneering activism and Kamala's transformative leadership, these trailblazers advance justice in diverse fields such as health, education, social justice, and cultural representation. They exemplify the modern pursuit of a world where all people are valued and supported.

Advocacy & Justice

John Amanam,

The first African hyper-realistic prosthetic artist, parallels the advocacy of Thurgood Marshall, who sought legal equity for all. By challenging Eurocentric standards in healthcare and providing prosthetic limbs that cater to the unique needs of Black and brown individuals, Amanam highlights the necessity for inclusiveness in medical solutions, aligning with Marshall's commitment to ensuring equal rights for marginalized communities.

David Dennis co-founded Cutoff Recycle

Addresses environmental sustainability which resonates with Tim Walz's focus on community empowerment. Cutoff's main goal is to recycle hair cut by hairdressers. Several tons of hair that were previously unused are now chemically treated to be transformed into liquid fertilizer and herbicide to meet the needs of the 15 million Tanzanian producers who cannot afford agricultural products. Dennis embodies the intersectionality of social and economic justice. His work reflects the interconnectedness of environmental stewardship and community development, echoing the legacy of leaders who advocate for comprehensive solutions. Connect with David at info@cutoffrecycle.co.tz

David Clark III

Founder of the African Talent Outreach and Mentorship Program, is tackling period poverty in Rwanda by producing washable sanitary pads and offering menstrual education. His initiative has supported over 500 girls this month, helping them avoid missing an average of 60 school days annually. Each hygiene kit, costing $25 and lasting up to two years, promotes health and education.Clark's work reflects a commitment to social equity and aligns with Kamala Harris's advocacy for addressing systemic barriers. It also embodies W.E.B. Du Bois's belief in education as a means of empowerment, ensuring access to opportunities for all individuals. Connect with David at https://atomorw.org/

Sherie Cabezas

Sherie Cabezas's work aligns with the values of Ethel and Kamala through her commitment to advocacy, equity, and restorative justice. Just as Ethel Ray fought for dignity and support for the vulnerable and Kamala Harris champions systemic change, Sherie stands for the rights and well-being of those with developmental disabilities. After her son Justice was diagnosed with Isodicentric Chromosome 15 Syndrome (Idic(15)) at 15 months, she became a dedicated volunteer for the Dup15q Alliance, organizing the first Believe Walk in the Bay Area to build community and raise awareness. Her advocacy extends beyond her own family's journey, empowering others facing similar challenges. Sherie is also passionate about restorative justice, co-facilitating a victim-offender education group at San Quentin State Prison. She is now also navigating her son Theo's recent diagnosis of Type 1 Diabetes, advocating for awareness and raising funds through the Breakthrough T1D Walk to support treatment advancements.

Wanda Tucker

Wanda Tucker's journey to Angola as part of President Biden's historic delegation—the first U.S. presidential visit to Angola in 2024—embodies a deeply personal and collective quest for justice, historical recognition, and healing. As a direct descendant of Anthony and Isabella, among the first Africans forcibly brought to the American colonies in 1619, Wanda carries forward the legacy of her ancestors and countless unnamed Africans whose lives and stories were erased by slavery. Accompanied by her brother Vincent Tucker and their cousin Carolita Jones Cope, Wanda's presence highlighted the enduring connection between Angola and the United States, symbolizing the resilience and strength of those who came before her. Her work as an educator and her pilgrimage to Angola are acts of reclamation—restoring dignity, acknowledging history, and preserving the memory of those whose labor and sacrifice built this nation. Like Ethel Ray Nance and Kamala Harris, who have tirelessly championed equity and visibility for marginalized communities, Wanda ensures that the contributions and resilience of Black Americans remain indelible. Her inclusion in Biden's delegation underscores the profound importance of confronting this shared history and advancing justice as her journey and advocacy continues to inspire and unite.

Heather Courtney

Heather Courtney's advocacy for disabled individuals, particularly within communities of color, embodies an intersectional approach to justice that both Ethel and Kamala championed. As a disabled U.S. Navy veteran living abroad, Heather founded Black.In.Portugal and the Lisboa Melanin Collective to foster community empowerment. Her efforts to create inclusive spaces for marginalized voices reflect Ethel's dedication to advocating for underrepresented communities and Kamala's focus on ensuring that all people, regardless of background, are included in the fight for equity and justice.

Larry Jones

Larry Jones, a 32-year veteran of police work, has long been familiar with the challenges facing African American youth. After retiring, he dedicated his time to mentoring boys aged 12 to 18 through the OK Program of Oakland. This initiative, in collaboration with the police, schools, and the community, tackles high dropout rates, incarceration, and violence among young African American males. Leveraging his law enforcement experience, Larry builds trust between youth and police while providing guidance and support. His work with the OK Program of Oakland mirrors Ethel Ray Nance's focus on empowering Black communities and Kamala

Harris's emphasis on building trust and justice through community engagement. Larry's commitment to mentorship and positive change demonstrates a belief that true justice begins with support, guidance, and equitable opportunities for young people in the Oakland community.

Naky Gaglo

Naky Gaglo's work as a historian and founder of the *African Lisbon Tour (ALT)* is a testament to his dedication to challenging imperialist narratives and offering a new perspective on African history. By highlighting Portugal's often overlooked role in the transatlantic slave trade, Naky contributes to the vision of Ethel Ray Nance and Kamala Harris by ensuring that marginalized histories are brought to the forefront. His tours not only educate but also empower participants to confront uncomfortable truths, similar to Ethel's commitment to historical truth-telling and Kamala's focus on rectifying historical injustices.

Francis Joseph Gallego

Francis Joseph Gallego is a licensed clinical social worker specializing in oncology and also runs his own private psychotherapy practice. His work is deeply focused on marginalized communities, including people of color, women, Indigenous communities, LGBTQI individuals, and those grappling with chronic illness and mental health challenges. Francis's diverse experience includes community organizing, activism, social justice advocacy, and lived experiences as a consumer. Having grown up in both developing nations and the United States, Francis brings a global perspective to his work, deeply understanding the importance of intersectionality, diversity, inclusion, and representation. He is committed to dismantling systems of oppression and empowering people to embrace authenticity and healing as essential pathways toward equity and justice.

Health & Wellness

Beverly Daria Lochard

Beverly Daria Lochard's dedication to making yoga accessible to individuals with chronic conditions embodies the spirit of inclusivity and wellness that Ethel and Kamala have long championed. By creating spaces where everyone, regardless of physical ability, can experience healing and inner peace, Beverly reflects Ethel's advocacy for dignity and Kamala's focus on healthcare equity. Her work ensures that the benefits of wellness are distributed equitably, fostering physical and mental well-being for all.

Kachi Okoronkwo

Kachi Okoronkwo, a certified personal trainer and mental health warrior, advocates for holistic health by addressing both physical fitness and mental wellness. Her work focuses on destigmatizing mental health issues, particularly in communities of color, and ensuring that individuals have access to the resources they need to prioritize their well-being. Kachi's focus on the intersection of physical and mental health exemplifies a holistic approach to justice. Her advocacy for destigmatizing mental health in marginalized communities mirrors Kamala Harris's work in healthcare equity, and his dedication to ensuring everyone has access to wellness resources embodies principles of justice and equity.

Juliet Tumuslime

Juliet Tumuslime is a Ugandan entrepreneur who promotes environmental sustainability through bio-products that benefit both the environment and local communities. Her work fosters economic development while addressing environmental degradation, proving that sustainable practices can uplift marginalized communities and provide new opportunities for growth. Juliet's approach to sustainable development mirrors Kamala Harris's policies on environmental justice. By focusing on both economic empowerment and environmental stewardship, Juliet embodies the intersection of these critical issues, ensuring that justice is distributed equitably across social and environmental landscapes.

Ramzy Okyere

Ramzy Okyere, the founder of the Nkwa Foundation in Ghana, works to improve the lives of underprivileged communities by providing educational resources, clean water, and sustainable agriculture programs. His foundation focuses on addressing the fundamental needs of his community, ensuring that everyone has the tools to succeed. Ramzy's work with the Nkwa Foundation mirrors the fight for educational and economic equity. Like Ethel Ray Nance, who advocated for community empowerment, and Kamala Harris, who pushes for policies that address the root causes of inequality, Ramzy ensures that the most vulnerable have the resources they need to thrive.

Hellen Joram

Nomad Tanzania operates a collection of high-quality safari lodges across Tanzania, which are known for their commitment to sustainable tourism and community engagement. Hellen's work with the organization's community initiatives empowers vulnerable women through income-generating activities, aligning closely with Ethel's advocacy for women's rights and Kamala's focus on creating equal opportunities. By advising young women and promoting food security, Hellen uplifts women and creates pathways for their success, embodying the intersectional values of equity and support for marginalized communities.

Konboye Ebipade Eugene

Konboye Ebipade Eugene, a Nigerian artist, transforms discarded flip-flops into vibrant portraits, raising awareness about plastic waste since 2017. By using waste materials to create stunning artwork, Eugene encourages viewers to rethink their consumption habits and inspires positive change in the fight against plastic pollution. Konboye's work sits at the intersection of environmental justice and cultural representation, demonstrating how art can be a powerful tool for activism. Like Kamala Harris's environmental initiatives, Konboye's art calls attention to sustainability while ensuring marginalized communities are involved in conversations about justice and the environment.

Entrepreneurship & Innovation

Tammi Relyea

Tammi Relyea is the founder of BRA-série, a brand featuring innovative, stylish bra straps that empower women through personal expression and positive self-image. Before launching her brand, she worked with non-profits advocating for abused and neglected children, as well as in the entertainment design industry. Her commitment to giving back extended to volunteering her time for various community initiatives. Her current initiative, WO3, is a grassroots movement that promotes and supports women-owned businesses by uniting women from diverse backgrounds to make a collective impact. Tammi's work aligns with Ethel Ray Nance's legacy of advocating for women's rights and economic empowerment and Kamala Harris's focus on uplifting women and creating equitable opportunities for them to thrive. By building a community of support for women entrepreneurs and promoting representation, Tammi's initiatives foster empowerment, visibility, and economic independence for women, ensuring they have the tools to succeed in business and beyond.

Shiko Onyango

Shiko Onyango, founder of Tribal Trends and the Africa to the World Project, is a Kenyan fashion designer and artist empowering communities through sustainable fashion, art, and culture. Born in Nairobi, she blends traditional African craftsmanship with modern design, supporting over 1,000 artisans, stay-at-home mothers, and marginalized groups. Her work promotes economic empowerment and cultural representation, aligning with Kamala Harris and Ethel Ray Nance's legacies. *Africa to the World* showcases African talent globally, creating partnerships to elevate authentic narratives. By merging fashion, sustainability, and technology, Shiko highlights African innovation, celebrating its creative contributions worldwide.

Kalkidan Tadesse

Kalkidan Tadesse's creation of Ethiopia's first biodegradable sanitary pad, *Happy Pads*, addresses period poverty and promotes sustainable practices, aligning with Kamala's advocacy for reproductive justice and Ethel's focus on women's health and dignity. By ensuring access to safe and affordable menstrual products, Kalkidan contributes to a more equitable future for women and girls in Ethiopia.

Art, Media & Representation

Acynthia Villery

Acynthia Villery, the first Black female rodeo announcer with the Bill Pickett Invitational Rodeo, is a trailblazer in a traditionally male-dominated and predominantly white sport. Her work exemplifies the intersection of race and gender, inspiring young women and people of color to pursue careers in fields where they have historically been excluded. Acynthia's remarkable achievements will be further recognized in 2025 when she is inducted into the Black Cowboy Hall of Fame, cementing her legacy as a transformative figure in rodeo history. Additionally, she is the first female to be inducted into the Black Cowboy Museum in Rosenberg, Texas, founded by Larry Callies, highlighting her groundbreaking contributions to the sport and beyond. By breaking these long-standing barriers, Acynthia creates space for others to follow in her footsteps, reinforcing the importance of visibility and representation in advancing equity. Her pioneering presence in the rodeo world challenges deeply entrenched norms, much like Ethel Ray Nance's groundbreaking role as a Black woman in law enforcement and Kamala Harris's trailblazing ascent to the highest levels of American politics. Acynthia's advocacy for representation aligns with Ethel and Kamala's shared vision of a world where every individual can break through barriers, proving that when one person succeeds, it opens doors for many others to follow.

Abdulrahman Abel & Nigel D'Souza

Abdulrahman Abel and Nigel D'Souza, photographers and filmmakers, use their art to amplify the stories of marginalized communities and bring attention to environmental and cultural issues. Their work captures the beauty and resilience of these communities while challenging stereotypes and providing a platform for voices often silenced or misrepresented. By focusing on cultural representation and environmental justice, Abdulrahman and Nigel embody the principles of intersectionality and demonstrate how art can drive social change. This aligns with Ethel Ray Nance's advocacy for Black voices and Kamala Harris's efforts to champion equity and inclusion, ensuring that historically marginalized narratives are not only heard but celebrated and honored.

Paul A. Greene

Paul A. Greene, producer of *Just To Live: The Black Butterfly*, a documentary, embodies the principles of advocacy, equity, and intersectionality championed by Ethel Ray Nance and Kamala Harris. As a photojournalist/documentary photographer, Greene aims to visually answer the question, "What happened?" While he captures events as they unfold, he believes filmmakers can exercise cinematic liberties to explore the "why it happened" in greater depth. Through his documentary, Greene examines Baltimore's African American population as the "wings" of a butterfly, a symbol of beauty and resilience in the face of systematic inequalities. His work illuminates the historical and ongoing traumas that shape Baltimore's identity, advocating for a profound understanding of the social and economic injustices that define the city. This, he hopes, can spark processes that address some of these entrenched issues.

Greene's commitment to "question everything" aligns with Ethel's dedication to truth-telling and Kamala's transformative policies, advancing the ongoing struggle for justice and inclusivity.

Education & Cultural Preservation

Asha Wilkerson

Asha Wilkerson, a life coach and healer, emphasizes the importance of emotional wellness and personal empowerment, particularly for women of color. Her work focuses on helping women heal from trauma, navigate life's transitions, and reclaim their power in both personal and professional spaces. Asha's focus on healing and empowerment reflects an intersectional approach to justice, where mental health, gender, and race intersect. Her work aligns with the broader fight for gender and racial equality, echoing the efforts of both Kamala Harris and Ethel Ray Nance to uplift women of color and ensure that their voices are heard in spaces where they have traditionally been excluded.

Selamawit Seyoum

Selamawit Seyoum, an advocate for individuals with special needs, focuses on creating inclusive spaces that address the unique challenges of marginalized communities. As the parent of a child on the autism spectrum, Selamawit's personal journey led her to write *"Food Matters: Unlocking the Autism Food Plate,"* a comprehensive guide that explores the connection between nutrition and autism. Her book provides practical advice on managing allergies, understanding food sensitivities, and implementing casein-free and gluten-free (GFCF) diets to support children's well-being. Selamawit's advocacy demonstrates an intersectional approach by addressing the overlapping needs of race, disability, and socio-economic status, ensuring that every child can thrive. Her work continues the legacy of Ethel Ray Nance and Kamala Harris by promoting equity and support for the most vulnerable in society.

To learn more about the other amazing podcast guests who are making a difference in the world, visit Instagram: @connectingwithkarennance

Epilogue

Carrying the Torch Forward

The Unfinished Journey of Justice

The journey chronicled in these pages is a testament to the power of perseverance, courage, and vision in the face of profound adversity. From Ethel Ray Nance's pioneering activism in Minnesota to President Kamala Harris's trailblazing ascent to the highest office in the United States, this book weaves together a tapestry of interconnected lives and legacies, united by the same unwavering commitment to equity and justice. It's a story of bridges built across time and geography, connecting Minnesota to California, past to present, and struggles for racial, gender, and social justice that transcend generations.

But this narrative is far from complete — it is merely a chapter in a much larger, ongoing story that we all have a role in writing. This legacy of equality and justice has been shaped not just by prominent figures like Ethel and Kamala but also by countless others — modern trailblazers, advocates, and changemakers — each contributing their own light to illuminate the path forward. In the previous chapter, we explored how individuals like Abdulrahman Abel, Nigel D'Souza, Heather Courtney, and others continue to expand the vision that Ethel and Kamala championed, using their talents and platforms to advocate for underrepresented voices, dismantle systemic inequalities, and build a more inclusive future.

Ethel Ray Nance's life embodied the idea that justice is not a destination but an ongoing process—a relentless pursuit of a better world where everyone's humanity is recognized, valued, and protected. As a Black woman navigating the deeply segregated and inequitable landscapes of the early 20th century, Ethel knew firsthand the complexities of fighting for dignity and inclusion in a society that often sought to marginalize her very existence. Yet, she persisted, not just for herself but for all those who would come after her. Her belief in the interconnection of various struggles—whether they centered on race, gender, economic, or social justice—laid the foundation for what we now call intersectionality long before the term existed.

The torch she carried has been passed on, each new bearer adding their own light and purpose. President Kamala Harris and Vice President Tim Walz have taken up this torch in a modern era, shaping policies and leading movements that seek to transform the values Ethel cherished into tangible realities for countless Americans. Their work—from advocating for racial equity and reproductive rights to uplifting Native American and LGBTQIA+ communities—reflects a commitment to ensuring that no one is left behind in the quest for justice. Together, they are expanding the bridges that Ethel and so many others began building bridges that connect communities, honor legacies, and pave the way for those who will continue the fight.

Ethel's journey from Minnesota to California and her unwavering dedication to justice were acts of courage and vision that echo through my own life and the lives of countless others. Her story reminds us that true change is rarely swift or easy. It demands patience, resilience, and, above all, hope. It requires us to confront uncomfortable truths, to hold our society accountable, and to challenge the systems that perpetuate inequality. It calls us to dream of a better world—not just for ourselves but for future generations who will inherit the fruits of our labor.

As the Harris-Walz administration work begins, we are witnessing history being made in real time. Their efforts to reshape the social and political landscape of this country are a continuation of a legacy that began long before either of them took office. It's a legacy of refusing to accept the status quo, of pushing the boundaries of what's possible, and of daring to envision a nation that lives up to its promise of liberty and justice for all.

But the work of justice is far from complete. For every victory, there are new challenges; for every bridge built, there are gaps yet to be crossed. We must remain vigilant, steadfast, and courageous in the face of opposition. The history of Ethel Ray Nance teaches us that progress is not linear—it is a series of struggles, setbacks, and breakthroughs. It is the collective effort of many voices, each contributing their part to a symphony of change.

Let us honor the legacies of those who came before us by continuing to fight for a world where justice is not a privilege for the few but a right for all. Let us keep building bridges—across communities, across generations, and across differences—so that someday, the vision of equity, inclusion, and true freedom that Ethel Ray Nance dreamed of will be fully realized.

This is our moment to carry the torch forward, to add our own light to the flame of justice, and to ensure that its glow reaches every corner of society. In doing so, we pay tribute to the past, celebrate the present, and lay the groundwork for a future where all people, regardless of their race, gender, sexuality, or background, can walk across the bridges we have built together.

Yet, the torch does not rest solely in the hands of elected officials or public figures. It belongs to each of us. As I,

Karen Nance, continue my work as a lawyer, mediator, private investigator, podcast host, and advocate, I am reminded daily of the power we all have to shape the world around us. Whether we are standing in a courtroom, sitting in a classroom, organizing in our communities, or simply speaking out against injustice when we see it, we are each part of a collective movement toward equity and inclusion.

This book is a tribute to the lives and legacies of Ethel Ray Nance, Kamala Harris, Tim Walz, and all those whose names may not be known but whose work is no less significant. It is also a call to action. It urges us to recognize that we stand on the shoulders of giants, and with that recognition comes responsibility. The bridges they built, the paths they cleared, and the doors they opened are not endpoints but gateways to future progress. Our job is to carry forward what they started, to expand these bridges, and to ensure that the light of justice shines ever brighter.

So, as we turn the final page of this book, let us remember that we are not closing a chapter but stepping into the next phase of this ongoing story. The journey from Ethel Ray Nance to Kamala Harris—a legacy of equality and justice—is one that will continue to evolve with each new voice that dares to speak out, each hand that reaches across divides, and each heart that commits to building a more inclusive and equitable future.

Let us honor the legacies of those who came before us by continuing to fight for a world where justice is not a privilege for the few but a right for all. Let us keep building bridges—across communities, across generations, and across differences—so that someday, the vision of equity, inclusion, and true freedom that Ethel Ray Nance dreamed of will be fully realized.

This is our moment to carry the torch forward, to add our own light to the flame of justice, and to ensure that its glow reaches every corner of society. In doing so, we pay tribute to the past, celebrate the present, and lay the groundwork for a future where all people, regardless of their race, gender, sexuality, or background, can walk across the bridges we have built together.

The journey continues. The torch is in our hands. Let's illuminate the path forward.

APPENDIX A

EDITORIAL ROOMS OF
THE CRISIS
70 FIFTH AVENUE, NEW YORK

NATIONAL ASSOCIATION
FOR THE
ADVANCEMENT OF COLORED PEOPLE

W. E. BURGHARDT DU BOIS

September 26, 1922.

Miss Ethel May Ray,
209 East 5th Street,
Duluth, Minn.

My dear Miss Ray:

    I thank you very much for your activeness in behalf of the Dyer Anti-Lynching bill. We seem to have been temporarily defeated but we shall keep on. I am showing your letters to the Secretary, Mr. Johnson.

                Very sincerely yours,

                W. E. B. DuBois

WEBD/PF

APPENDIX B

NATIONAL OFFICERS

PRESIDENT
MOORFIELD STOREY

VICE-PRESIDENTS
ARCHIBALD H. GRIMKÉ
REV. JOHN HAYNES HOLMES
BISHOP JOHN HURST
ARTHUR B. SPINGARN
MARY B. TALBERT
OSWALD GARRISON VILLARD

NATIONAL ASSOCIATION FOR THE ADVANCEMENT OF COLORED PEOPLE
70 FIFTH AVENUE, NEW YORK
TELEPHONE WATKINS 8098

JAMES WELDON JOHNSON,
SECRETARY
WALTER WHITE,
ASSISTANT SECRETARY

EXECUTIVE OFFICERS

MARY WHITE OVINGTON
CHAIRMAN OF THE BOARD
J. E. SPINGARN, TREASURER
DR. W. E. B. DU BOIS,
EDITOR OF THE CRISIS
ROBERT W. BAGNALL,
DIRECTOR OF BRANCHES
WILLIAM PICKENS,
ADDIE W. HUNTON,
FIELD SECRETARIES

September 27, 1922.

Miss Ethel May Ray
209 East 5th Street
Duluth, Minn.

My dear Miss Ray:

    I am acknowledging receipt of your most interesting letter with enclosures of September 7 to Dr. DuBois. This would have been done sooner had it not been for the fact that I have been out of the city and only returned yesterday.

    May I tell you how deeply we appreciate the splendid work that you have done in getting such splendid letters written to Senator Nelson. I am quite sure that his awakened interest and advocacy of the Dyer Bill was due in no small measure to these splendid letters written by such eminent citizens of Senator Nelson's own state.

    I suppose that you know due to a filibuster by Southern Democrats the Senate was prevented from taking up the Dyer Bill before Congress adjourned last week. However, we have definite assurances from the Senate leaders that the Dyer Bill will be the first order of business and will surely be passed as soon as Congress reconvenes. It, of course, would have been much better had the Bill been passed before the November elections; but the activity of colored people throughout the country, similar to that done so effectively by you, has created a state of mind which will secure, we fully believe, the passage of the Bill. We are continuing our efforts and keeping up this work that this long fight shall terminate successfully.

    In accordance with your request we are returning the letters to you.

    With sincere appreciation, I am

        Very truly yours,
        Walter White
        Assistant Secretary.

WFW:B

www.ingramcontent.com/pod-product-compliance
Lightning Source LLC
LaVergne TN
LVHW051036070526
838201LV00010B/227